Y0-BPW-493

To

From

Sisters, Always

Compiled by Michele Gandolfi

Illustrated by Wendy Wegner

PP PETER PAUPER PRESS, INC.
WHITE PLAINS, NEW YORK

Sisters, Always

Sisters may share the same
mother and father but appear
to come from different families.

ANONYMOUS

Your siblings are usually the
first people besides your
parents to come to your aid in
time of trouble. They know your
admirable qualities, they know
your faults. They've seen you
during the good times,
but they've also seen you at
your very worst.

SHARI COHEN

The three of us are still best friends. If there were anyone in the world I could spend time with, do anything with, it would be my sisters. We have qualities that balance each other. Like Christy is so open and friendly and Kelly is cute and smart.

ERIN TURLINGTON

Jamie and I have run the gamut from tearing each other's hair out when we were kids, to ignoring each other, to being each other's best friend.

KELLY CURTIS,
about her sister, Jamie Lee Curtis

It all started when I realized I was the only kid on the block who didn't have a brother or sister. It was embarrassing. All the other kids had stories to tell, and I was jealous. So I nudged my parents and then just stayed out of their bedroom long enough until they had Goldie.

PATTI HAWN

The thing about closing the
age gap with your little sib is
that (a) it's inevitable . . . and
(b) it has its good points.
Andrea is every bit the sage,
world-savvy confidante that
I want in a best friend, and she
and I see eye-to-eye more
with every passing year.

FRANCESCA DELBANCO

Alice is the rock, the one you can call at three in the morning, and she'll always be ready to help in any way.

REBA MCENTIRE,
about her sister Alice Lynn Foran

[Our father] didn't like us
wearing makeup and we had
a curfew, some ridiculous hour
like ten o'clock, and if you
weren't in the house, you
usually got locked out. Us
sisters were always sticking
up for each other and sneaking
each other in the window
at night.

BETTE MIDLER

Geordie and Mary were able to
get away with murder because
if there was some upset about
the house I was usually the
cause of it. I was always the
instigator of strange things
that we did. Also, I usually took
the blame because, with my
dark mysterious looks, I
appeared the most guilty.

MARTHA GRAHAM

Where I go, she goes.

ROSA PONSELLE,
about her sister Carmela

Louisa dear
With love sincere
Accept this little gift from me.
It is with pleasure
I send this treasure
And with it send much love to thee.

Sister dear
Never fear.
God will help you if you try.
Do not despair,
But always care
To be good and love to try.

ANNA ALCOTT,
to her sister Louisa

I'll never forget the time Peter and I were streaking my sister's long, ash-blond hair with light blond and proudly demonstrating the new "weaving" technique we had just learned in beauty school, when my sister muttered, "Gee, it's amazing that all the hair is in the tinfoil and yet it's going to still have dark streaks."

FRAN DRESCHER

They all irritated me
occasionally beyond endurance,
with the sole exception of
Alice. She never irritated me.
She was balm to my soul.

EDITH HAMILTON,
about her sister Alice

[Sophia Loren and her sisters]
loved to climb on top of the
sturdy old kitchen table to per-
form. Sofia dreamed up plays
for them, and they also sang
and danced. Romilda taught
them how to make costumes
from tissue paper, and loaned
them lipstick and rouge to
make up with.

WARREN G. HARRIS

Now we have really come together as adults. [Volleyball] made me who I am. And I like who I am. . . . And I really like my sisters. It just gets better as the years go on.

BEV ODEN,
volleyball star

You hit her and I'll knock your
teeth down your throat.

DIANNE FEINSTEIN,
at eleven, to a group of boys
harassing her sister Yvonne

Sisters stand between one and
life's cruel circumstances.

NANCY MITFORD

The older daughter is married
off by her parents, the younger
daughter by her sister.

RUSSIAN PROVERB

[My mother] elevated her behavior as a model for the rest of us. Yet I can understand how Margaret's acquiescence made life easier for my mother, who struggled daily to get by.

JOY HARJO,
about her sister Margaret

When she came to see me, I was
not the same troubled girl she had
always known, the "crazy" one.
We laughed together sitting in the
sunshine as she exclaimed:
"You're not crazy at all. You never
were." She wanted forgiveness and
I was glad that all was forgiven,
that our sisterly bond could now
be sweeter, stronger—deeper.

BELL HOOKS,
about her sister

We're best friends.

DEBBIE ALLEN,
about her sister, Phylicia Rashad

I could never love anyone as
I love my sisters.

LOUISA MAY ALCOTT,
spoken by Jo, in Little Women

Sisters are our peers,
the voice of our times.

Elizabeth Fishel

I've always been a bit leery about explaining my love for my sisters in public because I don't want us to sound crazy, but there is a bond between us that goes beyond normal sisters. I think it comes from our love of God, from our parents teaching us to love each other unconditionally, and from sharing a business where we've helped each other and been there for each other.

LOUISE MANDRELL

I was very lucky to have two sisters who treated me like any normal sister and not like a deaf kid. They looked at me as a person, not as a handicapped person. Stacey treated me like any girl treats her nosy little sister, and Melissa was my best friend. My sisters (who are both married now with wonderful families of their own) added color and richness to my life.

HEATHER WHITESTONE

My sister La Costa was more like our mother than I was. I was a hell-raiser like Dad. And since La Costa was a mama's girl, she did more feminine things than I did. . . . La Costa was very close to our Grandmother Tucker, who was still living in Denver City, Texas. I think she inherited two things from Grandma: her candy-making talents and her entrepreneurial spirit.

TANYA TUCKER

I was moved to look at Sarah and realize that I did not know who she was. At the time, I annoyed her by repeating to her over and over, "You're my sister, you're my sister." I did not really know what I was feeling . . . It was a profound sense of distance from her, a keen unknowing of who this person walking beside me was, how we two, by pure chance it seemed, fit into the world together.

LUCY GREALY

We've shared everything.
It only seemed natural to
share this too.

JENNIFER HONE,
when she and two of her sisters all
gave birth on the same day

We heard a song,
we heard it in harmony.

MAXENE ANDREWS,
of the Andrews Sisters

We were never so close
as when we laughed.

RICHARD STERN,
about his sister Ruth

We still aren't storybook
siblings, but I think Jaime
knows now that I care. If I
didn't, I wouldn't have come
after her and dragged her home
(after she ran away).
And I guess if *she* didn't she
wouldn't have come.

DARCY LOCKMAN

By the time we were adults,
our lives were on three very
distinct tracks. Mother would
shake her head in bewilderment
and say to Father, "How did
we get three daughters
so different?" He would
merely smile.

FAITH ANDREWS BEDFORD

Whenever I try to live in another town, my phone bill rockets; and when I look carefully at the breakdown of the call times, I see that I make the largest number to my sisters between the hours of four and five p.m.— that is, after-school time. I am fifty, but I still have this habit, this longing to hear their stories of the day. I want them to make me laugh.

HELEN GARNER

We never had much sibling rivalry; in fact, we've never even had an argument. And once I got a little braver about crossing lines, I became quite fierce about protecting her at school and on the playground (and she did get into a few face-offs!). She was my first real girlfriend.

LONI ANDERSON

Sometimes I think I know
everything there is to know
about my sisters but this isn't
true. I talk about them too
much to strangers and worry
afterwards that I've left out
everything that is important.

GILLIAN MEARS

My sister Mary was a strong influence in my life at this time and she encouraged our wild imaginings. . . . She taught me beautiful poems, which I enjoyed reciting . . .

MINNIE PEARL

We've lived together most all of our lives, and probably know each other better than any two human beings on this Earth. After so long, we are in some ways like one person. She is my right arm.

SARAH LOUISE (SADIE) DELANY,
about her sister, Bessie

Teaching my sister to read, write, and count gave me, from the age of six onwards, a sense of pride in my own efficiency. . . . When I started to change ignorance into knowledge, when I started to impress truths upon a virgin mind, I felt I was at last creating something real.

Simone de Beauvoir

My sister Emily loved the
moors. Flowers brighter
than the rose bloomed in the
blackest of the heath for her;—
out of a sullen hollow in the
bleak solitude many and dear
delights; and not the least and
best-loved was—liberty. Liberty
was the breath of Emily's nos-
trils; without it she perished.

CHARLOTTE BRONTË

I *have* lost such a treasure, such a Sister, such a friend as never can have been surpassed,—she was the sun of my life, the gilder of every pleasure, the soother of every sorrow, I had not a thought concealed from her & it is as if I had lost a part of myself. I loved her only too well, not better than she had deserved, but I am conscious that my affection for her made me sometimes unjust and negligent of others.

CASSANDRA AUSTEN

The Francis twins were so deeply connected that, in telling each other's life stories, each sister would provide the same perspective on events whether she was talking about herself or about her sister. It was as if they were two distinct people with one shared memory bank. Their lives moved forward on parallel tracks, but then closed behind them like a zipper.

SUSAN SCARF MERRELL,
on Penelope and Paula Francis

We're different on the outside,
but amazingly similar on the
inside. Andi's the only person
I can be myself with.
The sister part is gravy.

LYNN PRICE

Only a sister can compare
the sleek body that now exists
with the chubby body hidden
underneath. Only a sister
knows about former pimples,
failing math, and underwear
kicked under the bed.

LAURA TRACY,
The Secret Between Us

My two sisters, Peggy Sue and
Crystal Bell, used to sing with
me too. We all were just called
the Loretta Lynn Sisters and
they never had a name of their
own. Then I sent them out on
their own. They didn't like it
too good at the time, but I did
it for their sake, not mine.

LORETTA LYNN

Marilyn (Monroe) and I are all eternally entwined like the strands of the double helix of the DNA. Marilyn and I made the journey, crossing that enormous sea of differences that had seemed to separate us. And it turned out that the longest distance we had to travel was from the head to the heart. During that journey we made together, she became my sister, my rival, and my friend.

SUSAN STRASBERG,
Marilyn and Me

I don't know why, but my sisters and I thought of ballet as a familiar scenario, not a profession. The three of us shared a bedroom, and the bed was our stage. Sug was the Teacher, Beverly was the Mother, and I was the Student, Daisy.

SUZANNE FARRELL

I stood on tiptoe to look at her.
She was big for a new-born
child and had a wispy corona
of jet-black hair so unlike the
rest of us. She looked very nice
sleeping peacefully and
I felt suddenly happy to
have a sister.

JACKIE CALLAS,
about her sister, Maria

We acquire friends and we
make enemies, but our sisters
come with the territory.

EVELYN LOEB

Claudia smiled sweatily and put up with all our mishandling. She was "the baby." She knew her place. Today she tells me how much she resented us. That was nothing to how much we resented her merely for being born.

ERICA JONG

I am very grateful to my sisters
for teaching me what I know
about people. For showing me
different ways to grow. For
never having to worry whether
they'll show up for me.

WENDY WASSERSTEIN,
on sisters Sandy and Georgette

One of the great advantages
we had is that we didn't grow
up in a family where there
were different expectations
based on gender.

SANDY,
Wendy Wasserstein's sister

I would take her as crew in our boat races, and I remember that she usually could do what she was told. She was especially helpful with the jib, and she loved to be in the winning boat. Winning at anything always brought a marvelous smile to her face.

EUNICE KENNEDY,
about her sister, Rosemary

I always regarded my sister
as a child who I, as the older
one, took care of. Even today
I still call her by the
diminutive "Lyudochka."

RAISA GORBACHEV

An older sister helps one
remain half child, half woman.

ANONYMOUS

I was five when my sister, Joni,
was born. I don't remember us
ever being close. Our lives were
always on separate tracks.
I vowed way back then, if I
ever had kids, I'd have them
close together.

VICKI LAWRENCE

My mama always told us we
were precious, so we believed
it. Also, we were always nice to
each other. Nobody could
understand that.

Florynce R. Kennedy

Most of the things that
come up are the good-sister
and evil-sister thing. I would
play the evil sister.

JENNIFER TILLY,
about her sister, Meg

I could go on and on about the
differences between my sister
and me. Despite them, we have
much in common. Growing
older has drawn us even closer.
Jinny's a much less public
person than I. She's very
content with the simple things
in life, and I'm not.

KITTY DUKAKIS

My most abiding memory of Lynny as a child is of the little girl who trailed behind us crying "Wait for me." Only when she too became a professional actress and had her second baby at the same time as I had my last did we transcend the gap and become close friends.

VANESSA REDGRAVE

And if you do see someone with a funny hat, you must not point at it and laugh, and you must not be in too much of a hurry to get through the crowds to the tea table. That's not polite either.

PRINCESS ELIZABETH,
to her sister, Margaret

You can't think how I depend
upon you, and when you're not
there the colour goes out of my
life, as water from a sponge;
and I merely exist, dry and
dusty. This is the exact truth:
but not a very beautiful
illustration of my complete
adoration of you; and longing
to sit, even saying nothing,
and look at you.

VIRGINIA WOOLF,
to Vanessa Bell

For when three sisters love
each other with such sincere
affection, the one does not
experience sorrow, pain, or
affliction of any kind, but the
others' heart wishes to relieve,
and vibrates in tenderness.
Like a well-organized
musical instrument.

ELIZABETH SHAW,
sister of Abigail Adams and Mary Cranch

Mummy certainly feels that
Margot loves her much more
than I do, but she thinks that
this just goes in phases!
Margot has grown so sweet;
she seems quite different from
what she used to be, isn't near-
ly so catty these days and is
becoming a real friend. Nor
does she any longer regard me
as a little kid who counts for
nothing.

ANNE FRANK

Babe was always the glamor
girl and I was always the
crumbum except when I was
away from her. Babe was
a perfectionist. Compared to
her I always felt insecure.

BETSY WHITNEY,
about her sister, Babe Paley

When we get to the rocking chair stage, we plan on living in very close proximity, either side by side or in the same house.

DIXIE CARTER,
about her sister, Midge

As you grow older your sister
becomes your best friend.
Gone are the reasons for
arguing. What remains
is the attachment.

CLAUDINE GANDOLFI